Copyright © 2017 Institute for Learning Environment Design
All rights reserved. This book or any portion thereof may not be reproduced or used in any manner whatsoever without the express written permission of the publisher except for the use of brief quotations in a book review.

Printed in the United States of America
First printing, 2017

ISBN: 978-0-9987545-0-5

University of Central Oklahoma
Institute for Learning Environment Design
100 North University Drive, Edmond, OK 73034

http://iled.uco.edu/

The Learning Designer's
Guide to LEM

TABLE OF CONTENTS

Learning Environments	6
Learning Environment Design	8
Learning Environment Modeling	10
Learning Environment Modeling Language	11
LEML Building Blocks	12
Building Block: Information	16
Building Block: Dialogue	18
Building Block: Feedback	20
Building Block: Practice	22
Building Block: Evidence	24
LEML Contexts	26
Context: Classroom	28
Context: Online Asynchronous	30
Context: Online Synchronous	32
Context: Experiential	34
LEML Actions	36
Action: Learner Action	37
Action: Facilitator Action	37
Action: System Action	37
LEML Notations	38
Notation: Start/Stop	40
Notation: Objective	41
The Modeling Process	42
Step 1: Plot Evidence	44
Step 2: Support the Evidence	46
Step 3: Add Context	48
Step 4: Add Actions	50
Step 5: Add Notations	52
Step 6: Share and Revise	54
LEML Patterns	56
Customizations	58
Summary	60
Example Models	62

LEARNING ENVIRONMENTS

Every day we interact in many places where people learn and receive information. You're interacting with one such space right now. Sometimes these environments help us learn; sometimes the environment kills our passion for learning. The bottom line is poorly designed learning environments result in poor learning experiences.

That's why learning environment design is so important. It's about helping people find their passion for learning. It's not just about helping our schools succeed; effective learning environments can help businesses grow, and communities thrive.

What do you think of when you hear the word "learning environment"? Do you think of a classroom? A building or campus? Maybe an online course? The most common associations are typically physical or formal spaces. While these are certainly learning environments, learning can also take place in less formal places like a web conference, social media, or video games, or in personal areas like an office, or a car.

An emerging trend is the combining of these formal and informal environments. Today's learning environments are increasingly more about the blending and connecting of learning spaces together.

LEARNING ENVIRONMENT DESIGN

Learning is arguably one of the most complex human phenomena to understand and support. Why is this? We all simply learn differently. What helps one person learn might hinder another person's learning. What motivates one person to learn may be a demotivator for another.

Learning something new is inherently connected to our past learning experiences, which are unique to each individual. This complexity and diversity of how people learn helps us answer the question of "Why learning environments matter?"

The design of the learning environment shapes our experience in the learning process. Learning environments matter because there is a fundamental and important connection between the environments where learning happens and the quality of our learning experiences.

To accommodate our unique perspectives, often the only aspect of a learning experience that can be designed is the environment, or the spaces and places where learning happens. There is an important connection between learning and learning environments.

LEARNING ENVIRONMENT MODELING

Learning environment design is technically an architectural process. Think about how an architect envisions and designs buildings. Learning architects design and build learning environments in much the same way. They often do this without many of the foundational tools used by building architects such as common, uniform practices and models that assist in the understanding, decision-making, and collaborating on the design of the learning environment.

Learning Environment Modeling, or LEM, addresses this issue by providing a simple system for designing learning environments that uses an easy-to-understand language combined with a visual modeling process. LEM is used for improving understanding, decision-making, and communication within learning environment design experiences.

Here's an example of a model created using LEM.

This model includes elements that make up the learning environment, context and linkages showing how those elements are related, and a general structure for the learning environment. The system or language used to create this model is called the Learning Environment Modeling Language (LEML).

LEARNING ENVIRONMENT MODELING LANGUAGE

All professions use a particular language and vocabulary that is unique to those in that professional community. In the field of architecture and engineering, the value of a shared design language is particularly important as it establishes the basis for communication and sharing knowledge.

In contrast, educational fields such as instructional design do not have a common language from which to build knowledge and solve design problems. LEML is a shared language specifically for designing and modeling learning environments.

LEML is a visual toolkit created to communicate learning environment design ideas and plans. LEML can be used for designing, evaluating, prototyping, and revising designed learning environments such as courses, training programs, and workshops. It helps to communicate how learning environments are designed in concise and consistent ways.

LEM produces visual diagrams of learning environments in much the same way an architect uses blueprints or site plans to show how a building is to be constructed. This visual approach creates a model for seeing how the learning environment is designed and can be used as a centerpiece for supporting design experiences.

The Learning Environment Modeling Language is made up of building blocks, which along with learning contexts, actions, and notations, can be configured to represent virtually any learning experience. In the next sections, we present a brief overview of these elements.

Information

Dialogue

Practice

Feedback

Evidence

LEML BUILDING BLOCKS

LEML Building blocks represent the components, or system nodes, of a learning environment. Each building block is composed of three components: type, description, and method. The building blocks in LEML make up the core ingredients of learning environments.

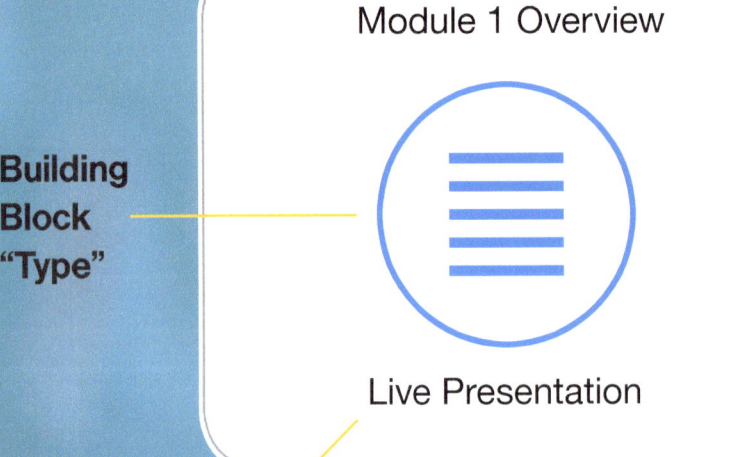

Description "What"

Module 1 Overview

Building Block "Type"

Live Presentation

Method "How"

Type

The building block type signifies the purpose or function of an element in a learning environment. LEML has five types of building blocks that can be configured to represent the design of any learning environment: Information, Dialogue, Feedback, Practice, and Evidence. Each building block type is represented by a graphical symbol in the middle of the building block.

Description

The building block description is listed at the top of the building block. The purpose of the description is to briefly describe the element.

For example, a description might read: "Module 1 Overview."

Method

The method is located at the bottom of each building block. The purpose of the method statement is to identify how the element is represented in the learning environment.

An example method statement for the Module 1 Overview might be "Live Presentation."

Building Block: Information

The Information building block represents a learning environment element that presents information to the learner.

Examples of Information might include articles, lectures, textbooks, images, videos, websites, or animations.

Building Block: Dialogue

The Dialogue building block describes communication, reflection, or collaboration elements within a learning environment. Dialogue can involve self-communication (reflection), communication with other individuals, or group communication.

Examples of Dialogue include classroom discussions, peer debate, group discussion, and reflections.

Building Block: Feedback

Feedback building blocks represent opportunities for instructors to comment or critique student work in a learning environment. The intent of feedback is enhancing performance and application of knowledge or skills.

Examples of Feedback building blocks might include diagnostic questionnaires, instructor feedback, and peer feedback.

Building Block: Practice

Practice building blocks provide opportunities to rehearse and practice skills in a learning environment. This building block is often used to represent formative assessment opportunities.

Examples of Practice might include application activities, problem sets, tabletop group exercises, individual assignments, and practice quizzes.

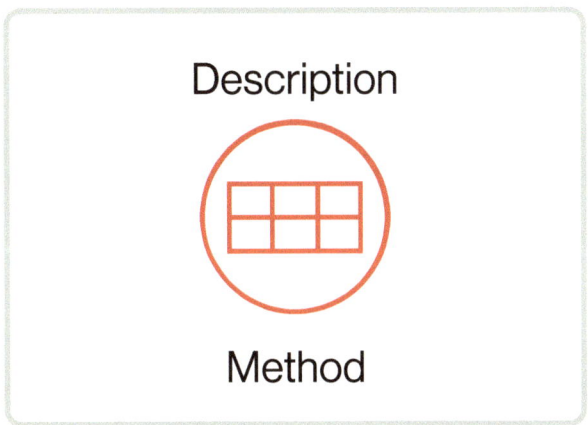

Building Block: Evidence

Evidence building blocks represent opportunities where evidence of learning is presented in a learning environment. Evidence is frequently associated with a stated learning outcome and is used to represent summative assessment opportunities.

Examples of Evidence include individual or group presentations, essays, individual or group projects, and examinations.

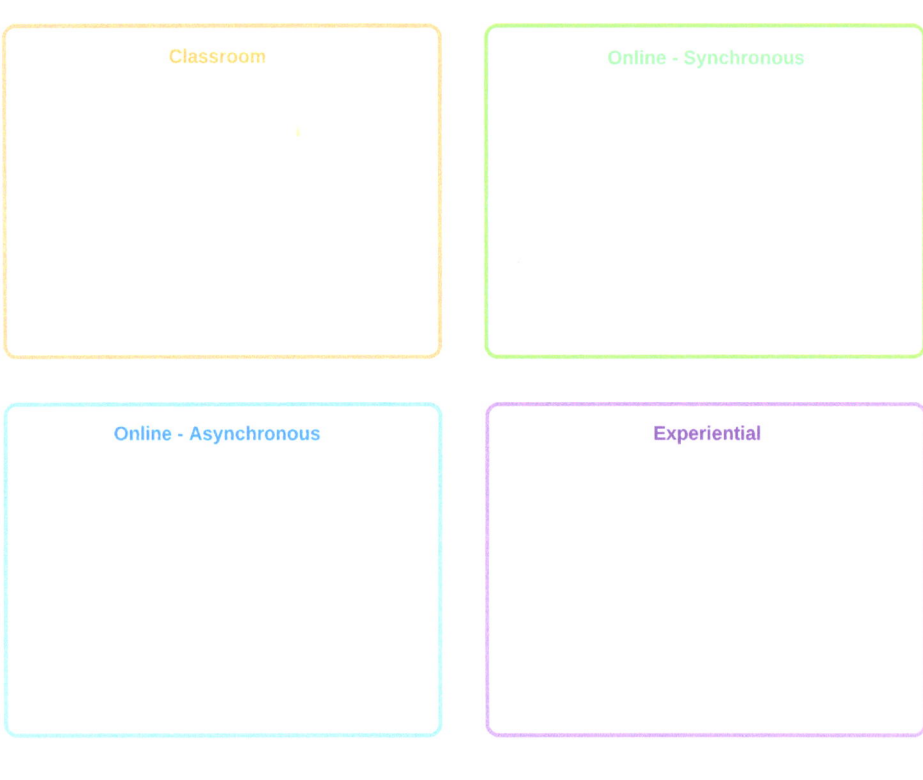

LEML CONTEXTS

The Contexts in LEML describe the spaces and places where building blocks reside in learning environments. There are four contexts represented in LEML: Classroom, Online Synchronous, Online Asynchronous, and Experiential. The contexts are represented by shaded container boxes.

The Contexts in LEML show the spaces where learning happens and where building blocks occur.

Context: Classroom

The Classroom context describes an interaction that occurs in real time within a physical learning space.

Examples of a Classroom context might include a formal classroom space, training room, or lecture hall.

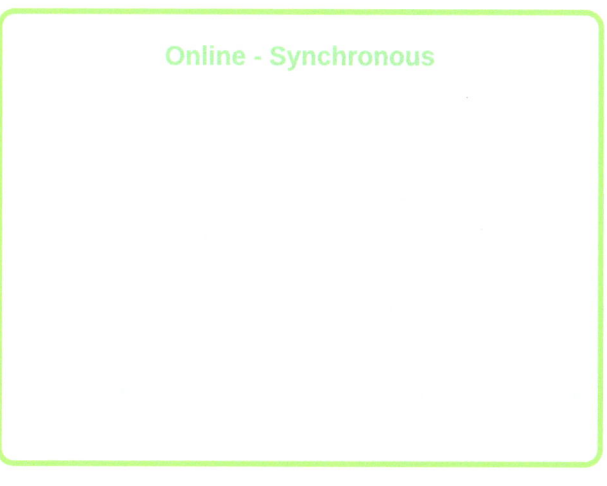

Context: Online Synchronous

The Online Synchronous context describes the elements that are delivered online in real-time.

Examples of Online Synchronous contexts might include online webinar platforms, instant messaging, and video chat tools.

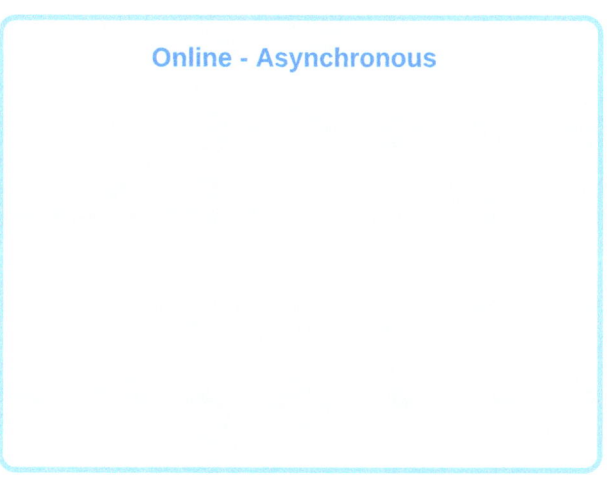

Context: Online Asynchronous

The Online Asynchronous context describes situations where interactions in the learning environment are conducted online at different times.

The most common example of this in educational settings is using a learning management system to access online courses. Many online social media platforms would constitute this type of context.

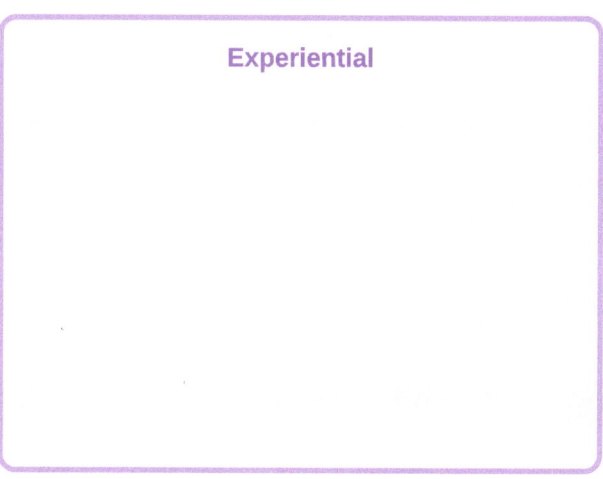

Context: Experiential

The Experiential context describes informal learning spaces where the experience plays a major role in defining the learning environment.

Examples of Experiential learning environments include learning commons, laboratories, workplaces, on-the-job training, and on-site field research sites.

LEML ACTIONS

The Actions in LEML identify the connections and transitions between building blocks and who or what is responsible for those transitions. Actions in LEML provide a way to show the flow and structure within learning environments.

There are three types of actions in LEML:
Learner Action, Facilitator Action, and System Action.

──────────────▶

Action: Learner Action

The Learner Action is used to identify transitions in the learning environment that are the responsibility of the learner.

Examples of Learner Actions include learners navigating through a self-paced online lesson, or a learner uploading an assignment to online assignment submission system.

•••••••••••••••••••••••••••••••••••••••▷

Action: Facilitator Action

The Facilitator Action is used to describe transitions that a facilitator or instructor manages within a learning environment.

Examples of Facilitator Actions include instructor provided feedback, and an instructor moving from one topic to the next topic in a workshop.

— ── ── ── ──▷

Action: System Action

System Actions are used to note automated or system-based actions within a learning environment.

Examples of System Actions include automatic notifications to students and conditional release criteria placed on content based on learner' performance on an assignment.

LEML NOTATIONS

LEML allows opportunities to annotate key elements in a learning environment model. Notations can be added to enhance the meaning and usefulness of the learning environment model.

While there are numerous possibilities for useful notations, there are two primary notation elements used: Start-Stop and Objective ID. Other notations can be added to learning environment models as needed to extend the meaning or to add explanation to models.

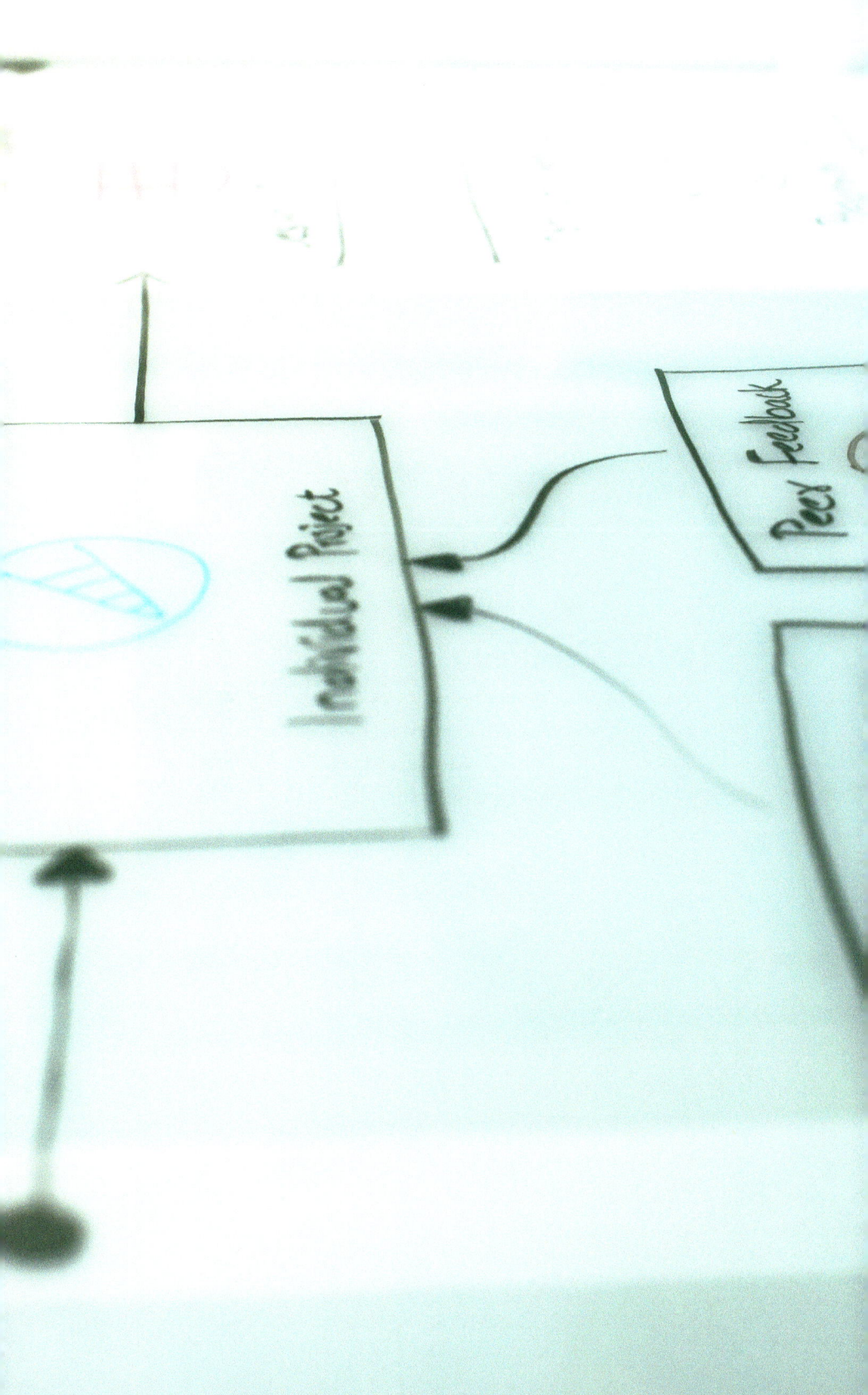

Notation: Start/Stop

The Start/Stop notation is used to represent start and termination points within a learning environment.

An example of this includes the start and end of an online lesson or workshop.

```
╭─────────────────╮
│                 │
│   Objective ID  │
│                 │
╰─────────────────╯
```

Notation: Objective

The second notation is the Objective notation. This notation is used to identify how a learning objective or outcome is represented in a learning environment.

An example of this might include identifying where in a learning environment demonstrates the achievement of a learning objective.

THE MODELING PROCESS

In the following section you will learn how to create learning environment models using LEM. Before we begin, it is important to point out a few tips that will help you use LEM effectively.

First, LEM can be used for two general purposes: diagnostic modeling and design modeling. Diagnostic modeling is used to create models from existing learning environments to better understand them and make improvements. Design modeling is used as a brainstorming-type tool when you are creating an entirely new learning environment.

Before you begin modeling, be clear about the major learning outcomes or vision for the learning environment; however, don't worry too much about specific learning objectives or steps.

Next, you should expect to go through many different versions and iterations when creating learning environment models. Try to avoid the goal of "perfection." LEM is intended to be a quick and easy-to-use communication tool; striving for perfection can be at the cost of innovation.

Finally, keep your ideas movable by using analog methods like sticky notes, whiteboards, and paper early in the modeling process and digital tools like diagramming software later in the modeling process once ideas are more solid. Keeping your ideas movable encourages collaboration and avoids commitment to ideas too early in a modeling process.

It is also important to note that there is no single defined process for using LEM. LEM is designed to support many different design approaches and philosophies by helping to enhance communication, collaboration, and shared meaning. Regardless of the process you may use, LEM serves primarily as a modeling and communication tool that can support various activities throughout the design experience. The following steps are a general outline and approach that you can use to get started with using Learning Environment Modeling.

So, let's get started.

Step 1: Plot Evidence

Plot Evidence building blocks based on the major learning objectives/outcomes. This involves writing what the learner will create in the learning environment as evidence that learning has occurred. The first step in creating a learning environment model involves defining the outcome of the learning environment.

Next, develop evidence blocks for each major learning objective/ outcome. Evidence building blocks represent the activity or outcome that will be created or demonstrated by a learner. You might think of Evidence building blocks as the summative assessment or result of a learning experience.

As an example, if you were to create a model for a lesson about how to ride a bike, the description for the evidence block would indicate the learner successfully rides the bike around the block without falling down.

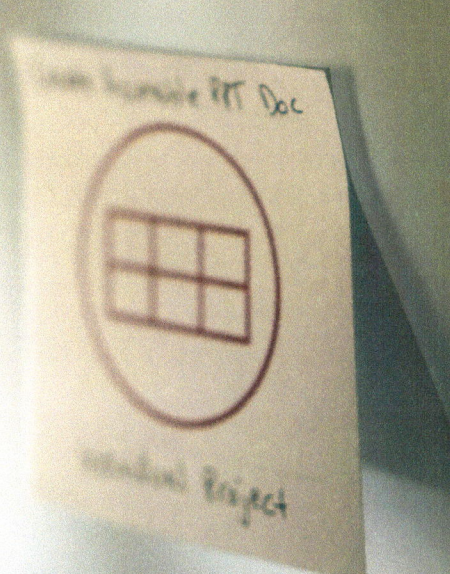

Step 2: Support the Evidence

Use the other four types of building blocks (practice, feedback, dialogue, and information) to support the achievement of the Evidence building block. Once the appropriate evidence building blocks are selected, begin using other building block types to develop experiences around them. This step is typically more organic in nature and involves micro-prototyping of design ideas. For example, you may choose to begin by adding a practice building block and then realize you need to go a different route.

Some designers begin by identifying the components needed to support the Evidence building block without developing any order of instructional plans. Other designers begin to form an order based on working through the design situation. Before moving on to the next step, you should have the evidence blocks and the blocks needed to support achievement of the Evidence building block on the idea canvas.

Step 3: Add Context to the Model

Once the building blocks are added to the model, you are now ready to add context elements. Context elements are boxes placed around building blocks as a method of showing the mode of the learning environment. Every building block should be contained in a context.

There are four contexts: classroom, online-asynchronous, online-synchronous, and experiential. Multiple contexts can be used in a given model to show how learning spaces can be combined.

Step 4: Add Actions to the Model

After the building blocks and contexts are represented on the canvas, the next step is to add actions to the model. Begin by arranging the building blocks in an order that supports your project. The goal here is to establish the model's flow and structure. Once you have this established, add actions to the model based on the role (learner, facilitator, or system) responsible for managing the transition between blocks. These arrows indicate the direction or flow.

For example, a transition between a classroom lecture and a discussion would use a dashed line with a hollow arrow as the facilitator is the one responsible for the transition. Alternatively, a learner completing a series of self-study modules would be represented by a learner action with an arrow to note this design in the model.

Step 5: Add notations and annotations

After actions are added to the model, it is time to add notations. Notations are used for start/stop locations and objective achievement. Also you may want to add annotations to support design and development activities. Adding annotations to learning environment models is particularly useful for supporting collaborative design and consulting experiences because it provides an opportunity to write notes or requirements from clients or other stakeholders within the context of the learning environment.

Create Accessible PPT Doc

Individual Project

Objective: Create Accessible Docs

Step 6: Share and revise as needed

After you create the first version of a learning environment model, you have the opportunity to present and share the model to others. This is a useful opportunity to collect feedback and ensure common understanding about the project for the design team and the client. The model also provides an active "idea canvas" for making revisions and adjustments to the design of the learning environment.

This step is critical to allow the models to grow and to improve. Sharing what you create with others allows you to practice communicating using the model while also learning from feedback.

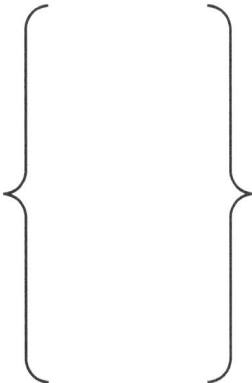

PATTERNS

Using LEM, designers can model patterns that occur in learning environments. For instance, an instructor may organize a classroom meeting a certain way every time the class meets. This is an example of a pattern that occurs in the environment. Another example might be an online course that uses modules to organize content and repeats certain sub-categories within each module.

Patterns can be simple, involving only a few building blocks, or they may be complex and involve a more involved sequence of elements. When modeling learning environments you may find that certain patterns have a repetitive nature based on the specific circumstances of the learning environment.

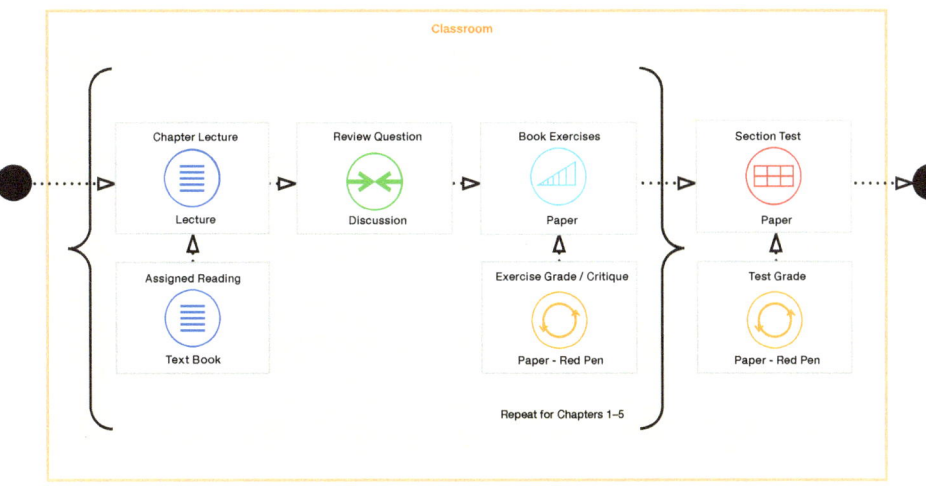

In this example, the instructor provides a lecture that is supported by a book chapter. An instructor led class discussion ensues. Students are then assigned practice exercises from the book chapter. These are graded and returned to the student.

After this learning pattern is repeated for chapters 1-5, students are tested summatively. The tests are graded with feedback and returned to the student. Brackets are used to signify the repeating pattern.

CUSTOMIZATION

LEM is not a rigid set of steps, but rather an overall approach to representing design ideas. Depending on the purpose for using LEM, you may choose to customize your approach.

For instance, if you are using LEM to create a model to better understand an existing course, you may work from an existing set of materials. In another situation, you may choose to begin with a certain feature or vision of a learning environment. If there is a specific type or style of feedback that needs to be incorporated in a learning environment, it may be preferable to start with those essential elements.

LEM is intended to be a flexible method for making effective design decisions. The ability to customize and personalize how LEM is used in design experiences is a useful feature. Customization allows for building shared meaning and enhancing the value of communication in design experiences.

When using LEM, you will encounter many different decisions on how to best model certain aspects of learning environments. While not specifically listed as a notation in LEML, a common method for identifying repeating patterns is to use open and closed brackets.

SUMMARY

So far you have discovered the different dimensions of learning environments and how to use LEM to communicate the way learning environments are designed. You learned about the different elements of the Learning Environment Modeling Language and the flexibility this approach provides as a planning and collaboration system. Finally, you explored how to use design patterns as a way of describing reoccurring strategies when designing learning environments.

EXAMPLE MODELS

This section of the book presents a series of examples and design patterns that you can use and modify to meet your needs. You will find these patterns and examples effective tools for exploring new ideas and implementing innovative design strategies.

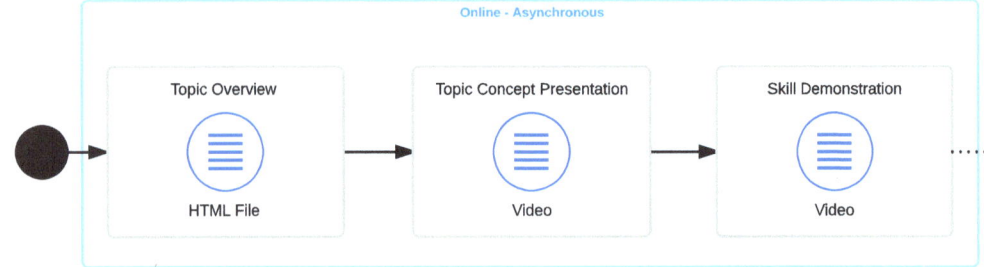

Blended Learning Model

Description: This model describes a way of designing learning experiences that incorporate both online experiences and classroom interaction to achieve a stated learning outcome.

Narrative: The class begins with a written topic overview, and videos presenting the topic concept and skill demonstration delivered via the web. Students then meet in the classroom to work on problem sets and to receive instructor feedback on their in-class work. The class returns to the online environment for a reflection discussion and submission of their individual-student problem set via Dropbox*.

Considerations for Implementation: This requires development of digital media and web content prior to implementing. It also requires effective facilitation skills to be able to manage groups working on different problem sets in the classroom environment.

*Methods may vary

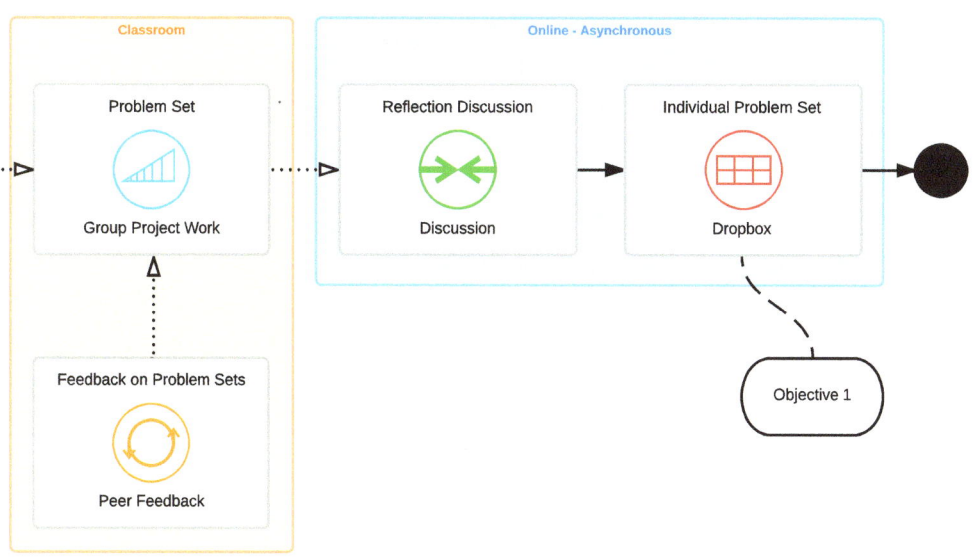

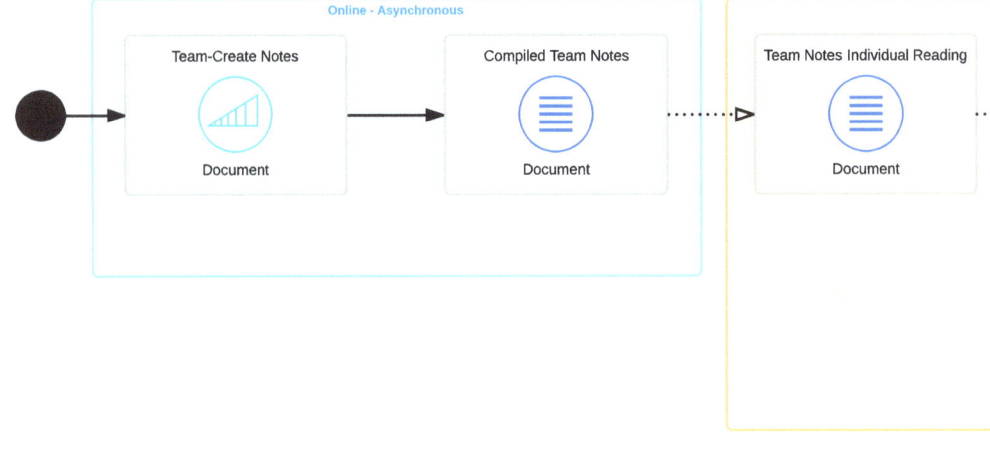

Feedback Focused Staff Meeting

Description: This model describes the organization of a staff meeting that relies primarily on interaction and feedback based on a provided set of informational notes.

Narrative: This staff meeting is built for brevity! Each individual team creates and compiles notes that are submitted to the meeting organizer via email. They are passed out at the beginning of the in-person meeting and time is given for attendees to read the notes. Attendees have the opportunity to ask questions to each team in turn and answers are presented and discussed by the team and by the group.

Considerations for Implementation: When implementing this model, you should allocate enough time to compile the meeting notes and clearly set expectations for how you intend to facilitate the meeting. Using meeting time for reading can be different for some people. Therefore, be prepared to model the behavior you would like to see to implement the approach.

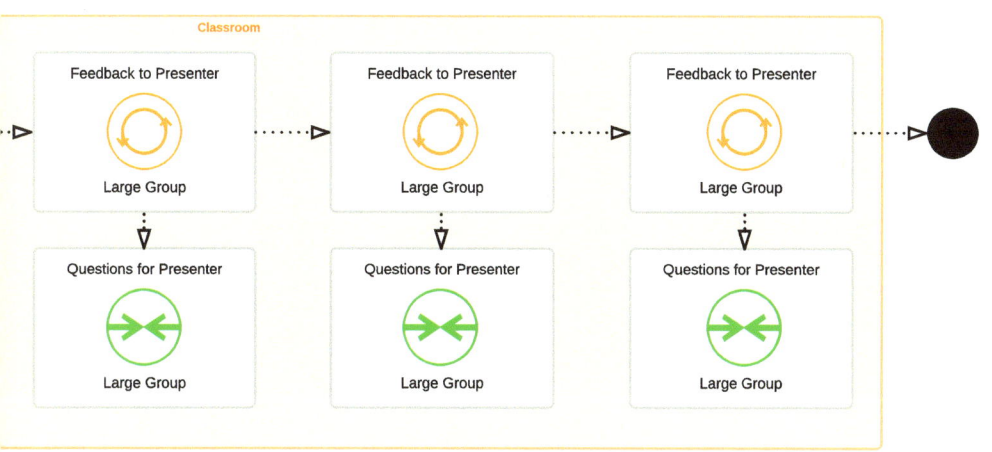

Knowledge-Based Project Development Environment

Description: This model describes a project development process augmented by a post-project "lessons learned" meeting and online knowledge management systems.

Narrative: Project goals are delivered via email in a requirements document. An in-person kick-off meeting provides team-building in the context of the project. Project development begins with support from an online project team forum that provides discussion and critique/feedback as well as a knowledge base with organized project resources. The project output is delivered and a meeting is held to provide "lessons learned" feedback from the team.

Considerations for Implementation: When using this model, you should clearly set team expectations and communicate those expectations with others. You should also communicate the value of capturing lessons learned in a shared knowledge base for future use.

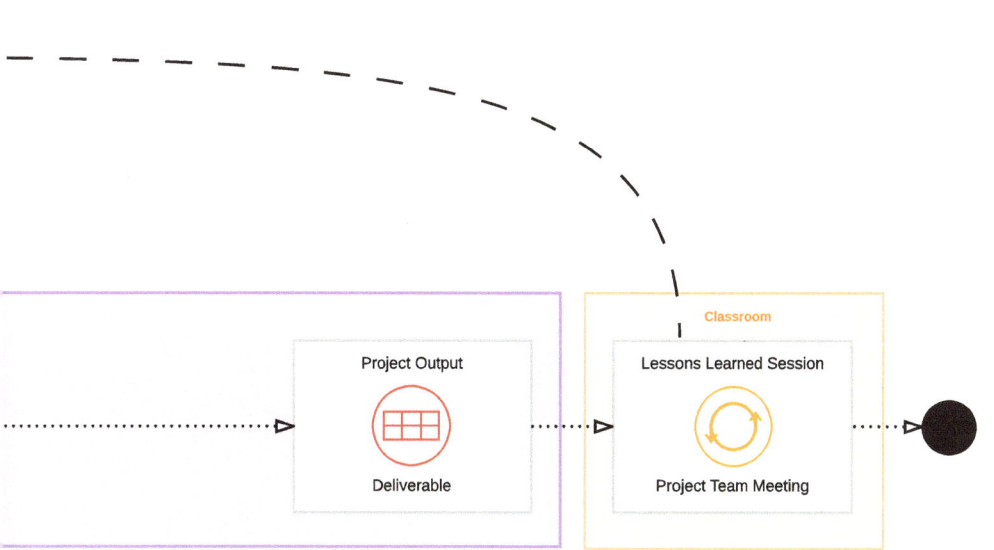

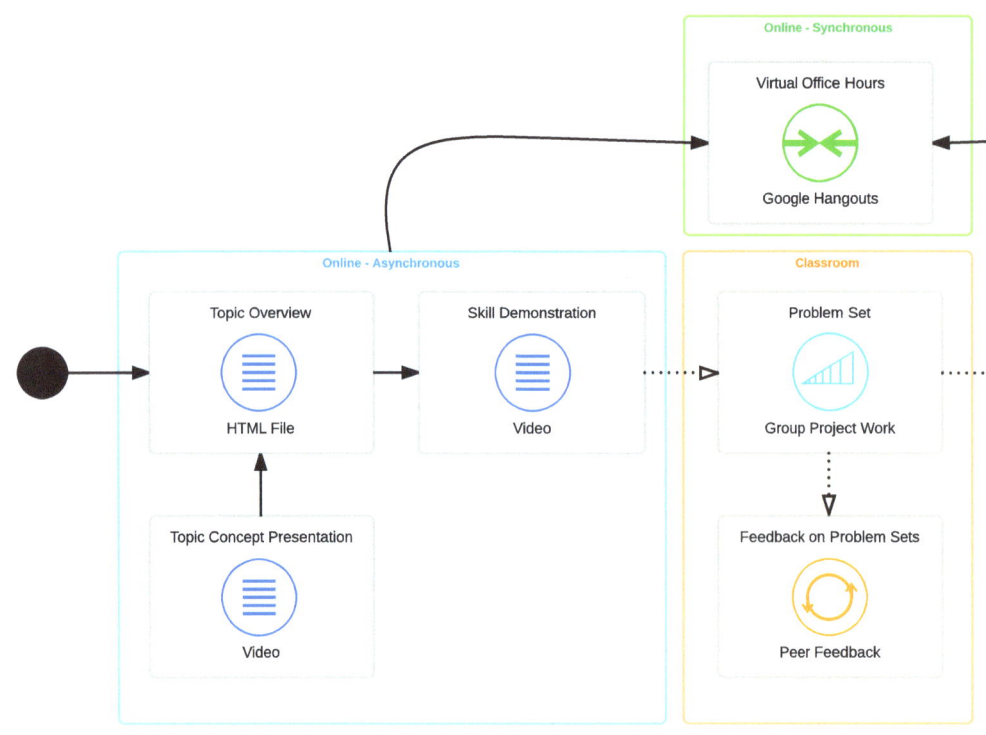

Multimodal Environment

Description: This model describes the integration of four different types of learning modes within a single learning exercise.

Narrative: Similar to the Blended Learning Example, this class begins with a written topic overview, and web delivered videos presenting the topic concept and a skill demonstration. Students then meet in the classroom to work on problem sets* and to receive instructor feedback on their in-class work. Next, students meet at a work-site to observe skills in action. Afterwards, learners participate in an online reflection discussion and submit their individual problem sets. The instructor maintains online office hours during the online portion of the class.

Considerations for Implementation: The primary consideration for implementing this model deals with consistent facilitation throughout the experience. The multiple contexts can provide some complexity for learners. The facilitator's role in this is to help the learner stay focused and oriented.

*Methods may vary

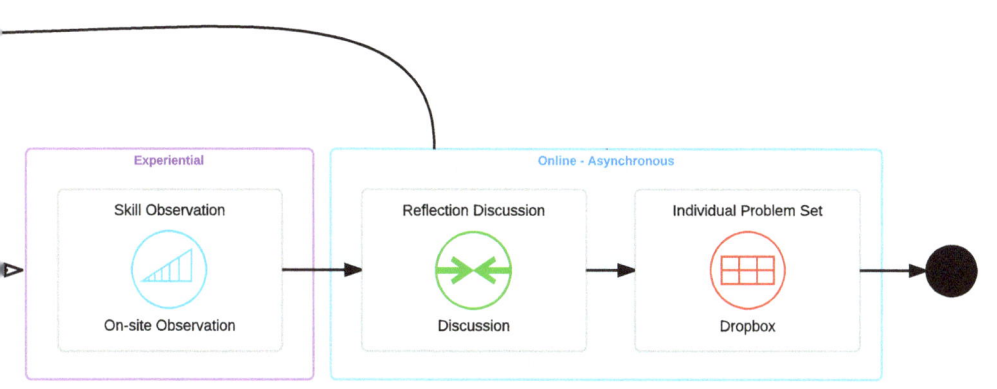

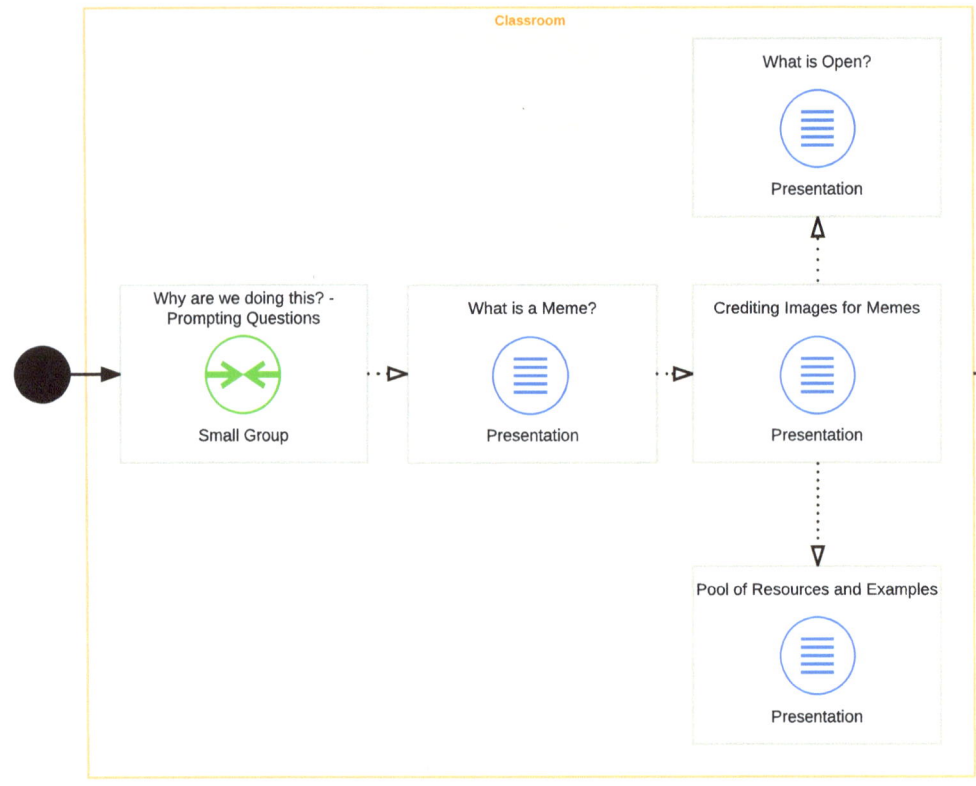

Open Content and PBL

Description: This model describes an open content and project-based learning interaction.

Narrative: Students begin by discussing the learning objective in the classroom context. They are then presented with content information also in the classroom. They then discuss their findings via an online sharing platform. They create a "How-To Guide" and receive feedback from both students and faculty via the platform. Evidence is demonstrated via a shared gallery showcasing their mastery of the content.

Considerations for Implementation: Instructors must have a good grasp of the course objectives and document them. Make sure that students understand content licensing (e.g. fair use), and open content curation. Finally, content quality is paramount – students should understand high quality content versus poor quality content.

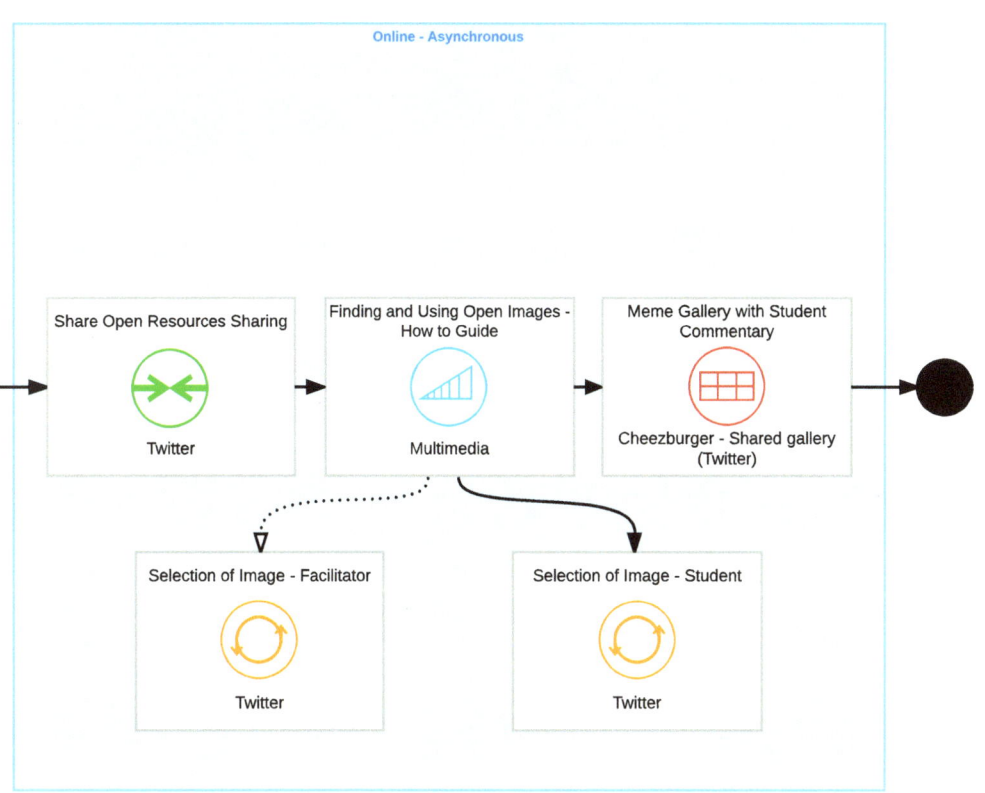

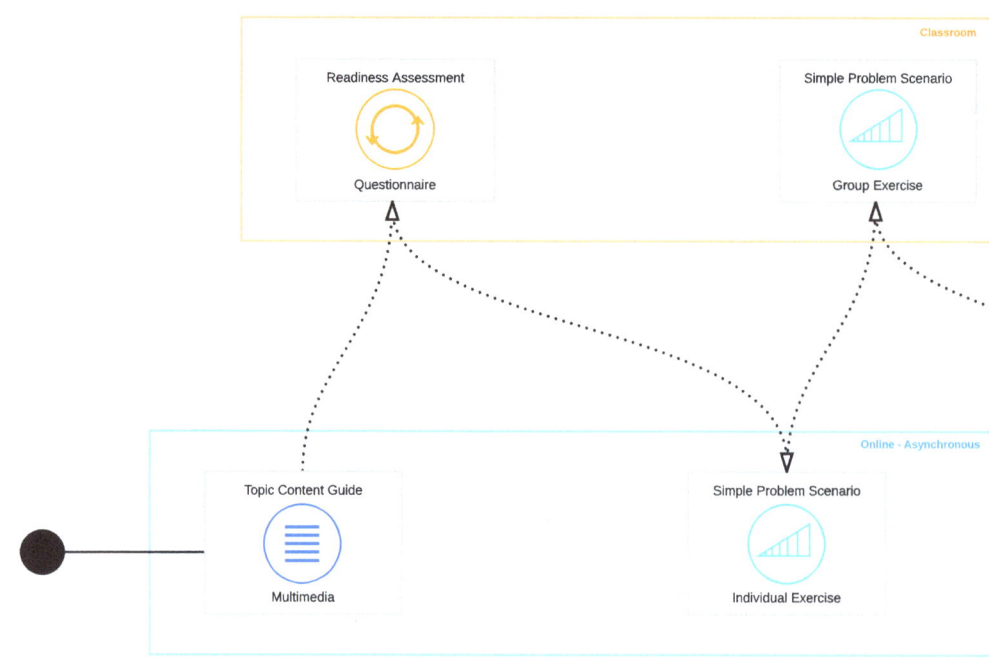

Team-Based Learning Instructional Activity Sequence

Description: Model of team-based learning instructional activity sequence.

Narrative: Students are presented with an online topic content guide. In the classroom, they complete a readiness assessment, then go online to solve a simple problem scenario. Back in the classroom, they form groups and solve another scenario. They repeat this pattern with a complex problem set: first online-solo, and then classroom-group. Review questions are presented and debated in an online discussion. Students return to the classroom to work in groups to solve the final problems*.

Considerations for Implementation: When using this model, you should clearly facilitate the transitions between the online and classroom spaces and that learners see the relevance of why each element is important in the overall experience.

References: Michaelsen, L. K., Knight, A. B., Fink, L.D. (2004) Team-Based Learning: A Transformative

Use of Small Groups in College Teaching. Stylus, Sterling, VA.

https://www.med.illinois.edu/facultydev/tbl/
ActivitySequenceGraph.pdf

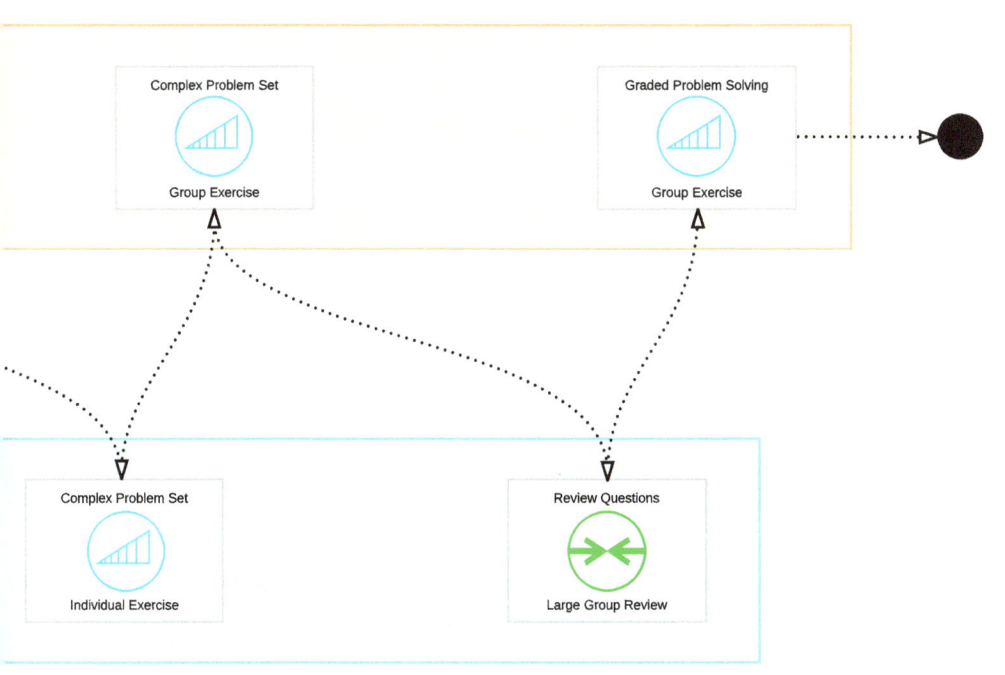

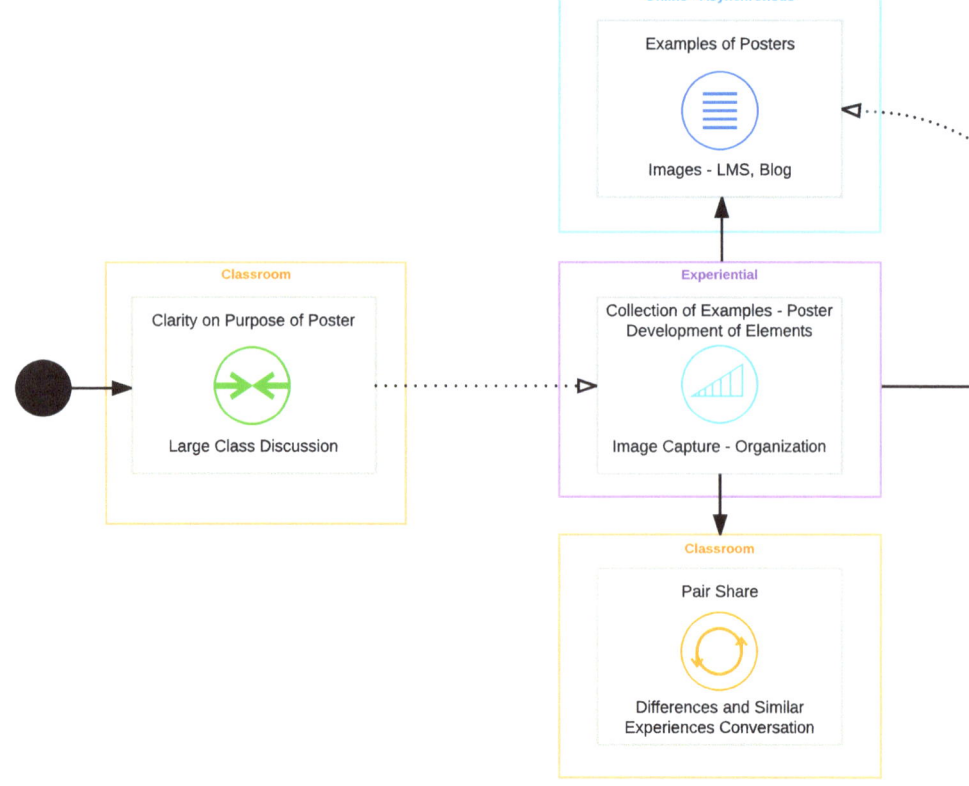

Rethinking Research Poster Presentations

Description: This model describes a new take on a research poster assignment.

Narrative: Students begin by discussing the assignment purpose in a classroom context. They then put together a collection of poster examples which is supported by online researching and peer discussion. Posters are presented in the classroom, but they are augmented with an online blog or website. Participants discuss and provide feedback on the presentation. Finally, a reflective video is recorded to provide introspection.

Considerations for Implementation: You should choose an important project - something of substance that is worth sharing like a research project or capstone - due to the level of organization and effort required for this learning environment. It will take a concerted effort to make sure all of the pieces come together.

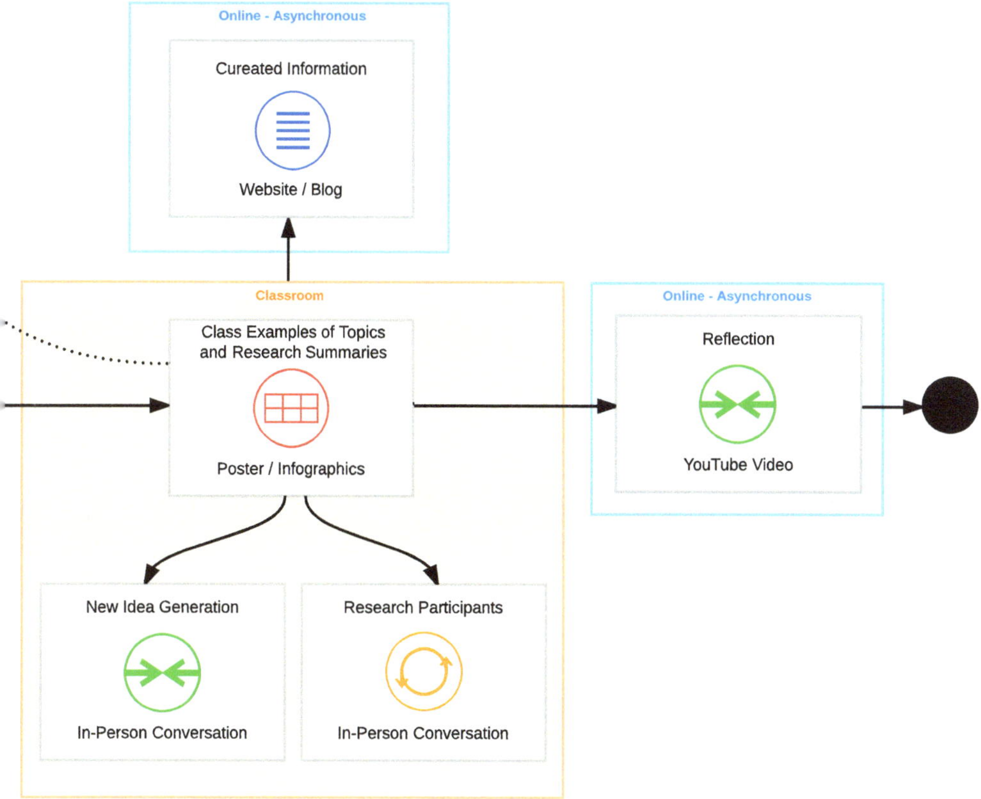

www.ingramcontent.com/pod-product-compliance
Lightning Source LLC
Chambersburg PA
CBHW041617220426
43671CB00001B/13